Koock Hyang Kim is on the pastoral staff team of a multicultural, independent evangelical church in central London. Originally from South Korea, Koock Hyang studied Genetic Engineering at university but was called to be a missionary to the UK, where she has served with a number of Christian organizations. At her church, she leads a ministry that helps people to find healing and wholeness in the Lord Jesus Christ and, ultimately, their purpose in His kingdom.

ALWAYS
AND
FOREVER

A self-counselling handbook

Koock Hyang Kim

Illustrated by

Christina Ng

Grosvenor House
Publishing Limited

This book is published by
Grosvenor House Publishing Ltd
Link House
140 The Broadway, Tolworth, Surrey KT6 7HT
www.grosvenorhousepublishing.co.uk

A CIP record for this book
is available from the British Library

ISBN 978-1-83975-384-8

Contents

Foreword

It is a pleasure to welcome *Always and Forever*, a book that I believe will prove to be of value to many people. The author, a deeply religious person herself, has provided Christian Ministry for many years. In addition, over the past fourteen years, she has developed her own methods of counselling and trained people in providing counselling. I have had many discussions with her about her work and my own as a psychiatrist and academic interested in the diversity of ways in which people round the world, in various cultural settings and from diverse backgrounds, deal with problems of the 'mind' — what we often call mental health problems. In hearing about her work, I have come to recognize the value of counselling that is religion-based, as well as its potential in helping people who are not particularly religious to help themselves, drawing on their own belief systems — and in my view we all have beliefs and values that inform our lives as human beings.

In this book, Koock Hyang Kim describes a system of self-counselling that she has developed, which a person requiring psychological help can use without the need for interacting with a specialist counsellor or therapist. Clearly, the person seeking help must apply the system by herself or himself, with the background here being a Christian belief system, but I reckon the basic approach can be adapted to other belief systems, and so this book could be a starting point for self-development for anyone sufficiently motivated to apply themselves to the task. The author herself has found that the method of self-counselling presented in this book has already helped many hundreds of individuals from a variety of backgrounds. And, most importantly, this is a book well suited to the multicultural societies of modern Britain.

Suman Fernando
Writer and former consultant psychiatrist
Author of *Mental Health, Race and Culture*, third edition (Macmillan International & Red Globe Press, London, 2010) and co-editor of *Global Psychologies: Mental Health and the Global South* (Palgrave Macmillan, London, 2018).

Preface

What do we do when we or someone we love faces difficulties? We try to find help, don't we? Sometimes solutions to problems come via counsellors but the field of counselling is complicated and vast, with many methods available. So, where do we turn? Is there anyone out there who can solve all our problems?

Let's say I know the Best Counsellor. He isn't asking for money. He isn't busy. He has all the time in the world for you. He can help you to solve your problems. If I offered to introduce him to you, wouldn't you leap at the opportunity?

If so, I'm glad you've opened this book. I do know the Best Counsellor and I'm very honoured to introduce you to Him, the One you can talk to at any time, throughout your whole life.

> Everyone who thirsts,
> Come to the waters;
> And you who have no money,
> Come, buy and eat.
> Yes, come, buy wine and milk
> Without money and without price.
> Why do you spend money for what is not bread,
> And your wages for what does not satisfy?
> Listen carefully to Me, and eat what is good . . .
> Hear, and your soul shall live;
> And I will make an everlasting covenant with you.
> (Isaiah 55:1–3 NKJV)

This book is a step-by-step guide to facing different issues with Him. You will learn how to receive solutions and healing with lasting effects. You can use this simple method detailed here for yourself or for people you'd like to help. I believe that, if you apply this guidance, you'll not only learn how to deal with problems but also find yourself connecting intimately with the Best Counsellor, becoming more like Him and able to see and approach life His way.

> Jesus said to him, 'I am the way, the truth, and the life.' (John 14:6 NKJV)

How the Best Counsellor has helped me

My life has completely changed since I met Him. I can confidently say that today is better than yesterday and tomorrow will be better than today. I have this confidence because the more time I spend with Him, the more I know Him intimately, which always leads to a fuller life.

I was someone who struggled under the burden of many problems: insecurity, rejection, jealousy, perfectionism, fear, anxiety, self-indulgence – you name it, I was weighed down by it. I was able to hide these problems from people and was doing so very well. Nevertheless, my heart was always in turmoil. When your heart isn't peaceful, it affects your health. I was eating healthy food and doing lots of exercise, yet I suffered continually from digestive problems. I was very religious, too, and I tried incredibly hard to sort my problems out but they just wouldn't go away. I kept facing problem after problem and struggle after struggle.

I wondered whether there was an easy and simple method that could help me to resolve most of my difficulties. I gradually found the answer after I learned to communicate with God, something that I discovered is only ever possible when I'm led by the Holy Spirit. Every step of Jesus Christ on earth was led by the Holy Spirit, so all the more reason for me to seek the Holy Spirit's guidance. It's a wonder that it took me so long to think of asking Him for step-by-step help with my problems.

> For all who are led by the Spirit of God are the sons of God.
> (Romans 8:14 NIV)

> If we live by the Spirit, let us also keep in step with the Spirit.
> (Galatians 5:25 ESV)

> Be transformed by the renewing of your mind.
> (Romans 12:2 NKJV)

> Teach me to do your will, for you are my God!
> Let your good Spirit lead me on level ground!
> (Psalm 143:10 ESV)

I want to emphasize here that the Holy Spirit is the Spirit of Truth and He will not speak on His own but speaks only what He hears (John 16:13-14). What He says to us is always aligned with the Word of God. So, through receiving ministry from God for many areas of my life, and seeing people set free during ministry over a number of years, He has shown me again and again that He is indeed our Best Counsellor.

God taught and led me at every step during different stages of my life, helping me to navigate tough issues and to mature spiritually. This book is God's teaching module for my life's journey: it can be yours too. After all, the more we receive God's ministry and come to know His truth, the closer we are to Him.

Is this method of healing for you?

Imagine that you're watching people in a swimming pool and you're someone who doesn't know how to swim. In fact, the thought of getting into deep water seems rather frightening. Some of the swimmers get out of the pool to come to talk to you. They say that they can float at the deep end; they say that they enjoy the water and don't fear it. You listen to them and you realize that you have a choice: you can speculate about the joys of swimming or you can get into the water and start to learn to swim. If you start to swim and discover that you don't like it, you can come out of the water. There's no pressure to learn to swim; whether you do so or not is entirely up to you.

Similarly, when you apply the method of healing offered in this handbook, you will see whether it produces good fruit in your life and whether it is of God or not. If you don't see good fruit, why persevere? I believe, however, that by following the guidance in this handbook, many personal problems can be resolved. Above all, following the steps in detail can help you to draw closer to God, to be increasingly sanctified by Him and to help you to depend on Him.

In and of itself, this method has no power. What it does is to encourage us to seek and trust in God for our healing. After all, we can trust that God will direct those who seek Him on to the right path. Hebrews 11:6 says that 'without faith it is impossible to please God, because anyone who comes to him must believe that he exists and that he rewards those who earnestly seek him'.

It is God who gives us understanding and revelation in Scripture. It is God who can give us the gift of discernment.

It is God who has solutions for all our problems. Let us trust the Lord who loves us, cares for us and protects us. He will direct us to the right path.

* * *

My sincere prayer is that *Always and Forever* will help you to begin a new journey. I hope that practising the ministry described here will become your lifestyle – one that will deepen your relationship with God as it allows Him to transform your life, leading to lasting, positive change.

> We all, who with unveiled faces contemplate the Lord's glory, are being transformed into his image with ever-increasing glory, which comes from the Lord, who is the Spirit.
> (2 Corinthians 3:18 NIV)

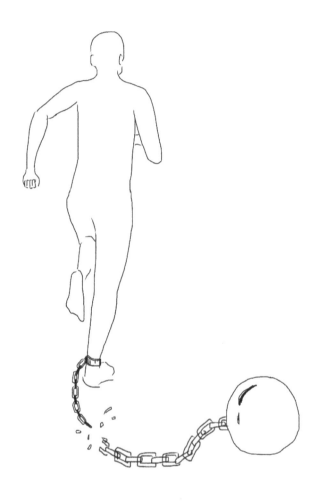

The truth sets us free

1
Problems?
No problem with the
Best Counsellor!

On the following pages are twenty examples of common difficulties we face. These examples are based on people's actual conversations during ministry with Jesus. During and after ministry with Him, they were set free from their problems. The conversations demonstrate how Jesus deals uniquely with individuals.

1. When I feel guilty because I keep doing wrong

3

4

2. When I feel overwhelmed at the thought of facing my problems

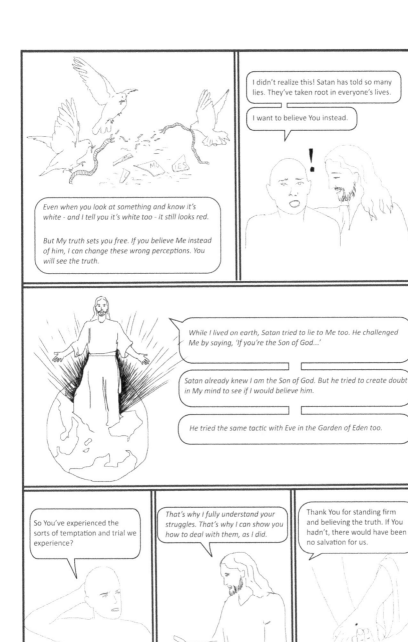

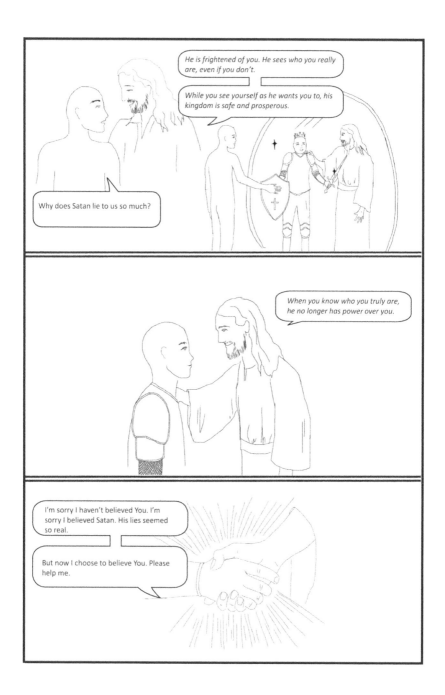

3. When I compare myself with someone

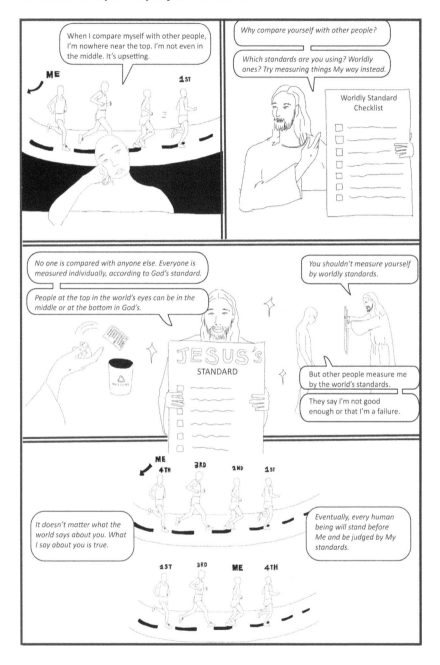

4. When I feel stupid

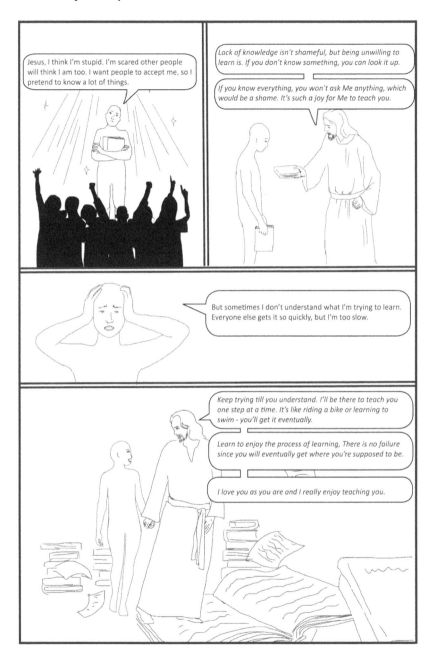

5. When I'm very competitive and don't want to share what I have

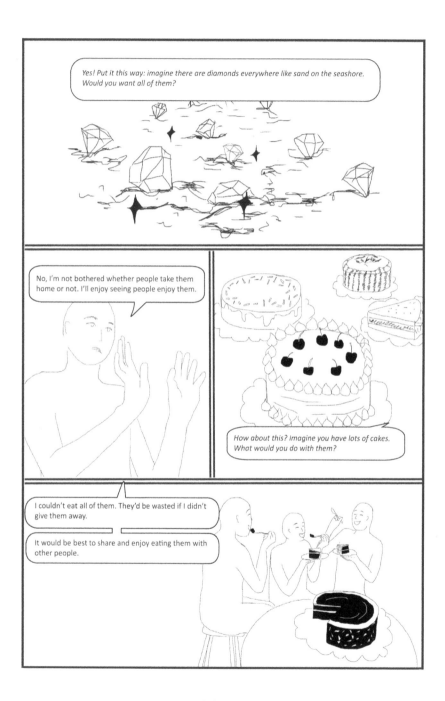

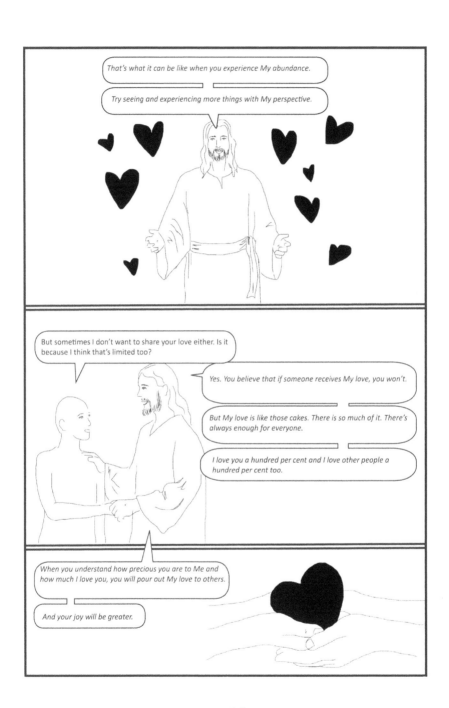

15

6. When my faith trembles

7. When I'm jealous because someone else gets the attention

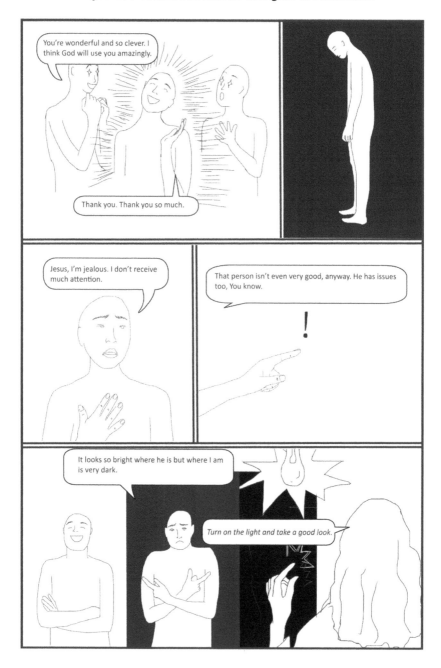

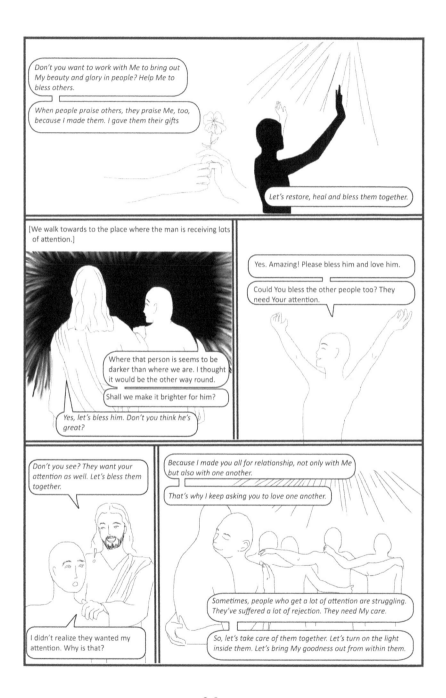

20

8. When someone hurts me

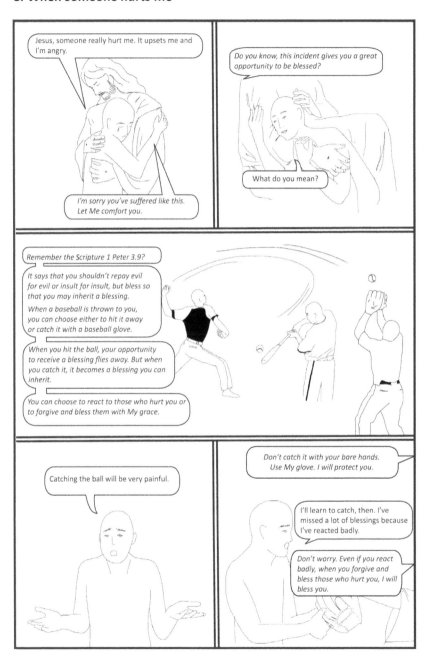

9. When I feel burdened by responsibility

10. When people label me

11. When God has promised to answer a prayer but I'm still waiting

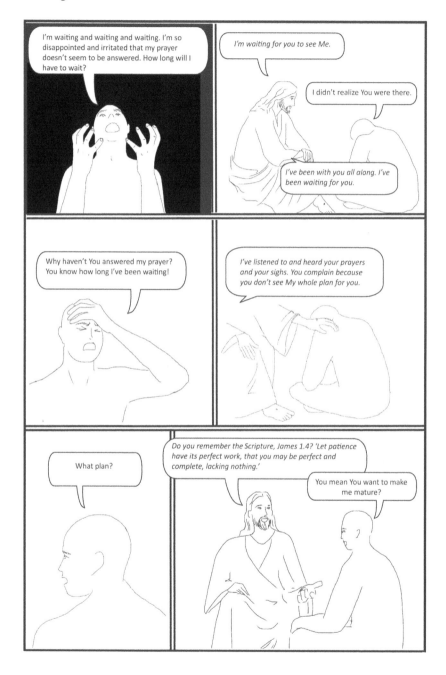

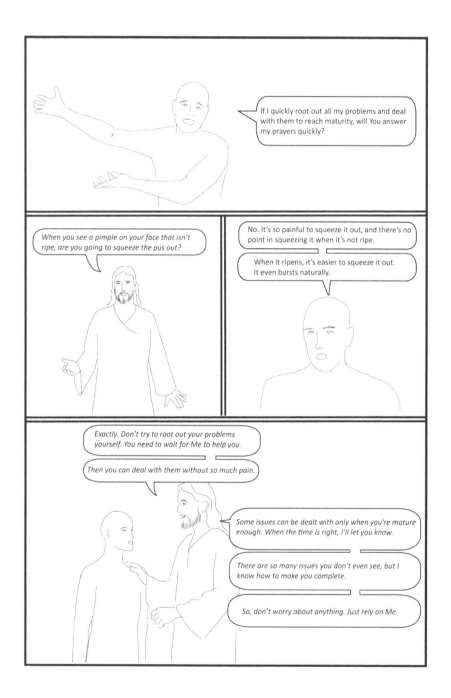

2 6

12. When I want to be seen as spiritually mature

13. When I'm struggling to submit to authority

14. When I'm upset by people who accuse me of doing wrong

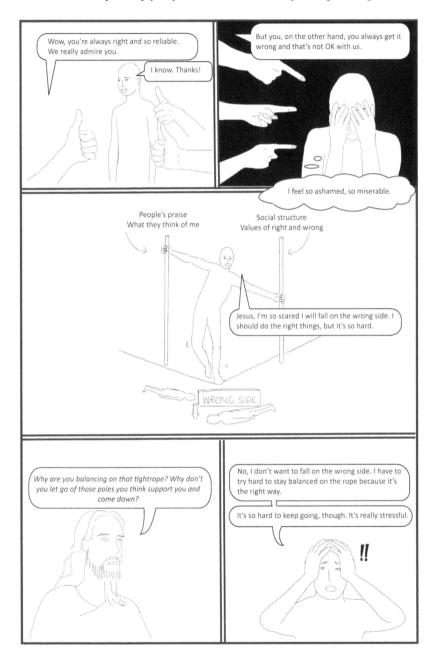

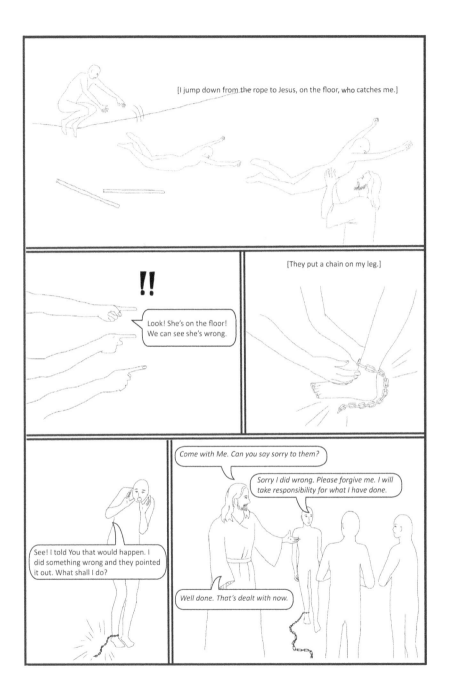

33

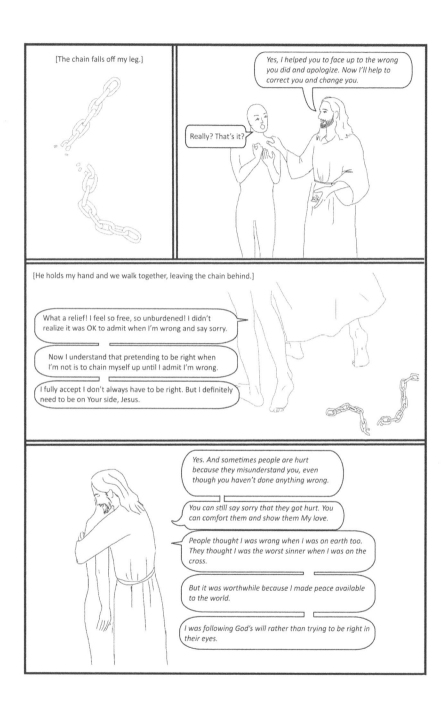

15. When I have a saviour mentality and need to help everyone who asks me

36

16. When I'm not treated as I think I deserve to be

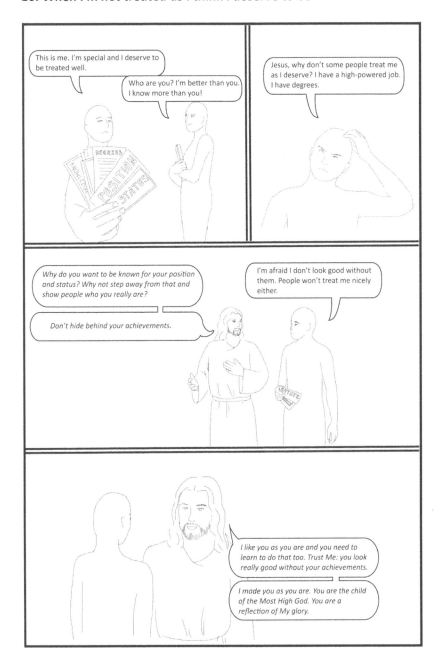

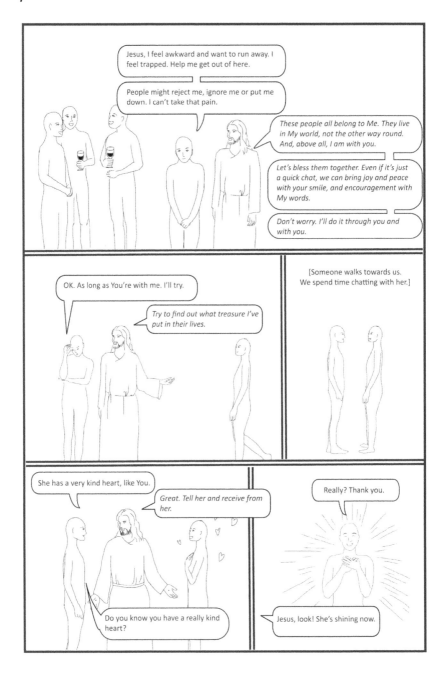

18. When I feel controlled by people

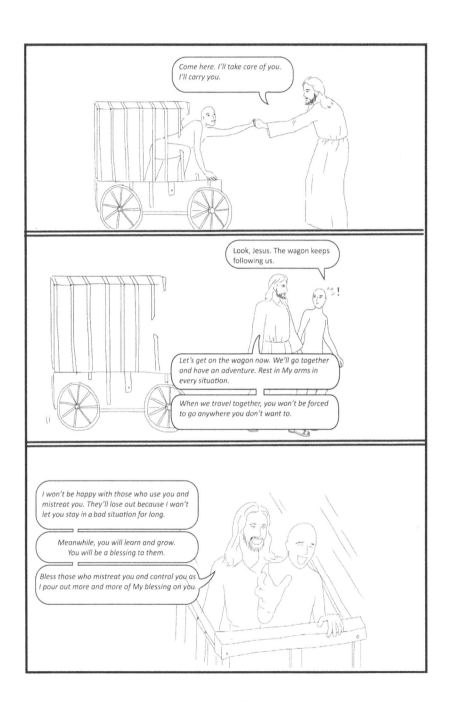

41

19. When I want to control people

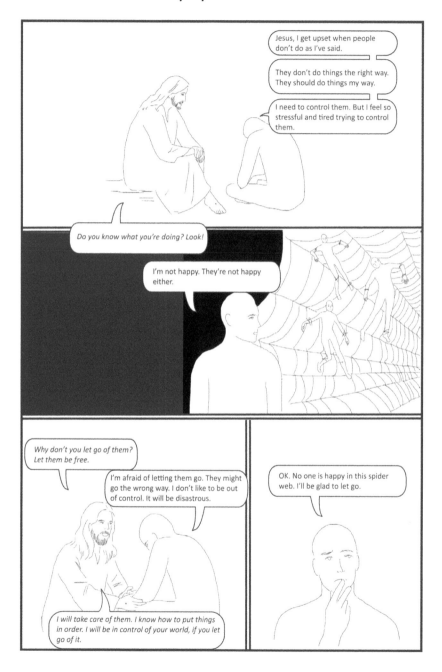

[As I let go of the situation and the people I controlled, I can see the spider's web changing into a rainbow, and God's hands are under the rainbow. People are riding on the rainbow and enjoying it, no longer stuck in the web. I also slide along the rainbow, which represents His promise that He will take care of them.]

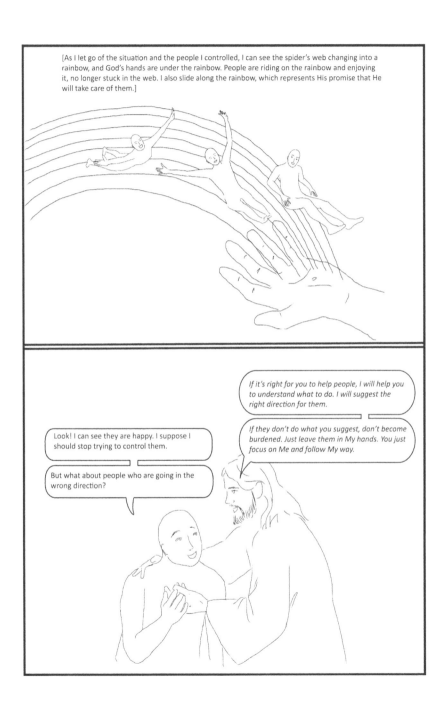

20. When I get nervous and don't feel confident about exams, interviews, presentations or performance

Open wide

2

Preparation

Before we look at how to deal with our problems, let's prepare by learning how to communicate with the Best Counsellor, the Person who can solve all our problems. There are a few steps we have to take to do this.

1. Accept Jesus Christ as your Saviour and Lord

God made us, and we were designed to be satisfied and fulfilled by Him. He cares for us, loves us and has provided everything for us. He wants to have a great relationship with us so that we can have an abundant life.

However, we want to be independent and do what we want. God respects our choice; He doesn't control us. The problem is that we often feel empty and struggle with other people and even ourselves. We can't seem to find real peace. We are far away from God, who is our source of abundant life.

Although we choose to be independent, God is loving and just. He still loves us and longs for a close relationship with us. The question is, how can He balance being who He is with dealing with this problem? His solution was to send His Son Jesus into the world. He lived the sinless and perfect life on earth that no human being could ever manage to live. When He died on the cross, He exchanged His holiness for our sinfulness to allow us to be holy. By doing so, He was punished instead of us.

Now the choice is ours. Jesus said that if we repent of our sins and believe in Him as our Saviour and Lord, He will be our righteousness and we will belong to Him. He will save us. He will be like a shepherd to us and we will be like His sheep, trusting Him, following Him and being safe with Him. What do you say to this offer? If you say yes, here is a simple prayer that you can pray:

Jesus, I thank You for dying on the cross for me. Thank You for giving Your life for me and for taking away the punishment for my sins. I accept You as my Saviour. I'm sorry for all the wrong things I've done and the things I haven't done that I should have done. Thank You for forgiving me and exchanging my sins for Your righteousness. Jesus, I accept You as Lord of every area of my life, surrendering all to You. Please be Lord of my spirit, my mind, my emotions, my will and my body.

2. Welcome the Holy Spirit to dwell in you

Jesus said that when we accept Him as our Saviour and Lord, the Holy Spirit will be sent to live in us. Here are some Scriptures in which Jesus talked about the Holy Spirit:

I will ask the Father, and He will give you another advocate to help you and be with you for ever – the Spirit of truth. The world cannot accept him, because it neither sees him nor knows him. But you know him, for he lives with you and will be in you. I will not leave you as orphans; I will come to you.
(John 14:16-18)

The Advocate, the Holy Spirit, whom the Father will send in my name, will teach you all things and remind you of everything I have said to you.
(John 14:26)

When he, the Spirit of truth, comes, he will guide you into all the truth. He will not speak on his own; he will speak only what he hears, and he will tell you what is yet to come.
(John 16:13)

You will receive power when the Holy Spirit comes on you.
(Acts 1:8)

Jesus breathed on His disciples, and said to them, 'Receive the Holy Spirit.'
(John 20:22 NKJV, adapted)

When Jesus was on earth, even He was led and empowered by the Holy Spirit. Are you willing to receive the Holy Spirit into your life? If so, here is a prayer to pray (as you pray, open your heart to receive the Holy Spirit, and be filled with Him):

Holy Spirit, I welcome You. Come and dwell in me. Let me be filled with You. Teach me, guide me, counsel me, convict me and empower me. Saturate me and transform me into Christ's likeness. Have Your way in my life.

3. Spend time alone with God daily to communicate with Him

Spend time reading and learning Scripture each day. Doing so feeds and nourishes our inner being because it helps us to get to know God more and grow in Him. Spending time with God daily should be our foundation: a strong building needs a strong foundation. The deeper the foundations, the taller a building can be. The more time we spend with God, the better we can deal with our issues.

In the Bible, Jesus says that those who believe in Him can hear His voice. Don't be afraid of hearing Him. And even if we mishear Him, He can redirect us. He longs to speak to us much more than we do to Him, so trust Him to speak to you. Whenever the Holy Spirit speaks, what He says always aligns with Holy Scripture; that is, you can always test what you hear against Scripture. Also, you will know whether what you heard is from God by its fruit: every good tree bears good fruit (Matthew 7:16–20).

We can sense God's speaking with our senses (hearing, feeling, seeing, tasting, smelling). Hebrews 5:14 says that we are to train our spiritual senses to discern both good and evil. So, let's always open our senses to communicate with Him, even if we wonder whether we're sensing our own thoughts and feelings rather than God. For instance, if I were to phone you every day, you would eventually recognize my voice without my having to say who I am, even though you might not have known who I was when I first phoned you. As we continue to communicate with God, we will eventually learn to recognize His voice. Remember, we belong to Him and can hear His voice.

One of the mistakes I made when I started talking to God was that I treated Him like a fortune-teller or an internet search engine. I just wanted to know things rather than to relate to Him properly. But He wants an intimate relationship with us. By practising listening to Him daily, we come to know Him as our Father, Counsellor, Best Friend and Almighty

God, growing in our 'heart knowledge', not just 'head knowledge', of Him.

There is one other important thing to note. Make sure that you are very honest with God about your thoughts and feelings. If you don't agree with Him, you don't understand what He says or you're not happy with Him or someone else, please say so. He will not judge us or get angry with us. Rather, He likes our honesty because it is a sign of our trust in Him. After all, He already knows what's in our hearts.

There are plenty of examples in the Bible of people who poured out their true feelings to God. In the Psalms, for example, David honestly expressed his raw feelings about his enemies. Psalm 3:7 says, 'Arise, LORD! Deliver me, my God! Strike all my enemies on the jaw; break the teeth of the wicked.' We often feel vengeful like this when people hurt us deeply, but how many people are able to express their pain and anger as openly as David did to God?

How do you express your pain and anger? Or do you bottle it up, feel ashamed of yourself? How do you deal with it?

Jeremiah was extremely honest about his feelings too. In Jeremiah 20:7, he says, 'You deceived me, LORD, and I was deceived.' Even though the prophet knew that God never actually deceives anyone, he told God exactly how he felt about the situation he was in.

Because of their honesty, God gave David and Jeremiah deeper revelations and a deeper relationship with Him. We too can trust Him by being honest. He will guide us step by step. However, after we have expressed our feelings to God, we always need to give Him a chance to speak to us. Remember, conversations with God are two-way discussions.

To illustrate how you can communicate with God daily, here are two guidelines, with examples, that have been helpful to others.

Guideline 1

(a) Choose a part of your daily Bible reading. Ask the Holy Spirit to show you what He wants to say to you through these Scriptures.

(b) Read the Scripture.

(c) Write down the words or sentences that you believe God is highlighting.

(d) Ask Him why He has highlighted this Scripture and note any answers.

(e) Communicate with Him honestly and make a note of the conversation:

ME:

GOD:

ME:

GOD:

ME:

EXAMPLE

(a) Choose a part of your daily Bible reading. Ask the Holy Spirit to show you what He wants to say to you through these Scriptures.

Numbers 6:22–27.

(b) Read the Scripture.

The LORD said to Moses, 'Tell Aaron and his sons, "This is how you are to bless the Israelites. Say to them:

'"'The LORD bless you and keep you;
the LORD make his face shine on you and be gracious to you;
the LORD turn his face towards you and give you peace.'"

'So they will put my name on the Israelites, and I will bless them.'

(c) Write down the words or sentences that you believe God is highlighting.
Peace: 'the LORD turn His face towards you and give you peace'.

(d) Ask Him why He has highlighted this Scripture and note any answers.
Answer: I always turn My face towards you. I want you to look at My face so that you can have peace.

(e) Communicate with Him honestly and make a note of the conversation.

ME: Do You mean You will give me peace as soon as I look at You? Is it that easy?

GOD: Yes. Try it.

ME: But what if I do wrong things? Will You still look at me then? If I were You, I wouldn't turn my face towards someone who hurt me.

GOD: When I see you, I see Jesus, your righteousness. So, just look at Me. Know that My face is always turned towards you. I will cleanse you and give you peace.

ME: Heavenly Father, thank You so much for Your love and care. Let me look at You.

I take some time to sense that His face is turned towards me until I feel peaceful.

ME: It's so peaceful knowing that You love me as I am and that You are for me, not against me.
GOD: When you worry, when you're guilty, when you're fearful, when you're doubtful, always come to Me.
ME: Yes, I will. Thank You. I love You.

I have had a conversation like this with God. Now, whenever I follow His instruction to look at Him, I feel truly peaceful.

Guideline 2

Ask God one of two questions: 'How do You see me?' or 'What would You like to say to me?'

God:

Me:

God:

Me:

God:

Me:

EXAMPLE

ME: God, how do You see me?
GOD: You are My twinkling star.
ME: I don't feel like a star at all.

GOD: I know how you feel about yourself but, the truth is, you are My twinkling star. You shine in My eyes and make Me smile.

ME: Why? Look at me. Sometimes I complain; sometimes I do wrong. I feel like a very dusty stone.

GOD: Whenever dust falls on you, I wipe it off and you become shiny again. I'm good at wiping away dust. Look – you're shining!

I can sense that I'm shining.

ME: Yes, I can see that. I didn't realize that You kept wiping me clean to maintain my shine. Thank You so much. I love You!

Basic Ministry

The enemy can influence our lives if, rooted in us, we have unforgiveness, sin, deep emotional pain or lies that we believe about ourselves, others and God, and so on. We use the Basic Ministry shown in the following flow charts to remove some of the enemy's influence upon our lives. Whenever we start to examine our issues or problems, we should ask ourselves the questions shown in the flow charts first and pray over them before we go into deeper ministry. The charts provide questions and sample prayers concerning:

- the Lordship of Jesus Christ
- forgiveness
- curses, vows and judgements
- emotional pain
- ungodly beliefs

The Lordship of Jesus Christ

Which *areas* are not under the Lordship of Jesus Christ?

- **My spirit**: relationship with God, Jesus and the Holy Spirit, my spiritual sensitivity, creativity, spiritual gifts and identity, and so on.

- **My soul**: thoughts and imagination, attitudes, beliefs, dreams, expression of feelings, reactions, defence mechanisms, coping mechanisms, behaviour cycles, decisions and choices, and so on.

- **My body**: health, sleep, rest, appearance, eyes and what I look upon, ears and what I listen to, mouth and what I say and eat, hands and all that I do and touch, feet and everywhere I go, sexuality and its expression, and so on.

- **My life**: family, possessions, perceived needs, time, work, ministry, leisure, plans, ambitions, future, destiny, all my relationships, and so on.

Pray: I confess I have not submitted myself to Your Lordship in [*name area*]. I repent of my sins. I choose to make You Lord over every area of my life. Even though it is impossible to change [*name area*] in my own strength, I can by Your grace.

Forgiveness

Whom do you need to forgive?

- The person who hurt you
- Yourself
- God

Pray: I choose to forgive [name] for [give details]. I release [name] into the freedom of my forgiveness. I bless [name].

Pray: I am sorry, God, for blaming You for [give details], even though You didn't do anything wrong. Please forgive me.

Pray: I release the forgiveness of God as I confess this sin [name it]. I release myself from guilt and shame.

In the Name of the Father, Son and Holy Spirit, I break all ungodly bondage of spirit, soul and body that has been established between me and the person who hurt me.

I ask You, Father, to cleanse me from all negative impacts and influences the bondage has had upon my life.

In Jesus' Name, I break every curse that has been established through this relationship and restore everything that was lost.

I ask You, Father, to place the cross of Jesus between me and the person who hurt me to stop the flow of everything ungodly between me and them, in Jesus' Name, amen.

Curses, vows and judgements

Have you made any curses, vows or judgements?

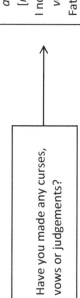

Pray: As a result of being hurt, I have allowed myself to harbour anger, resentment, bitterness and [*name any curse, vow, judgement*] in my heart against [*name*].

I now confess, repent of and renounce [*name curse, vow, judgement*].

Father, please forgive me and cleanse me. I ask You to break any curse on me or on any other person resulting from my judgements, in Jesus' Name, amen.

Emotional pain

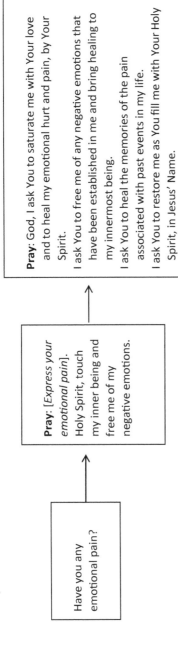

Have you any emotional pain?

→

Pray: [*Express your emotional pain*].
Holy Spirit, touch my inner being and free me of my negative emotions.

→

Pray: God, I ask You to saturate me with Your love and to heal my emotional hurt and pain, by Your Spirit.

I ask You to free me of any negative emotions that have been established in me and bring healing to my innermost being.

I ask You to heal the memories of the pain associated with past events in my life.

I ask You to restore me as You fill me with Your Holy Spirit, in Jesus' Name.

Ungodly beliefs

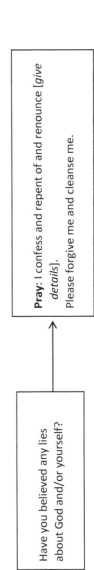

Have you believed any lies about God and/or yourself?

→

Pray: I confess and repent of and renounce [*give details*].
Please forgive me and cleanse me.

Jump in

3

Getting started with the Best Counsellor

Now let's learn about the ministry of the Holy Spirit. In it, you are led by Him throughout. Don't try to resolve things yourself. Instead, ask the Holy Spirit to help you and allow Him to lead you step by step (see Psalm 143:10; Romans 8:14).

In the past, I spent long periods of time trying to work out my problems myself, but I couldn't solve them and became even more confused. When I finally gave up and opened myself to the Holy Spirit, He asked, 'Would you like My help? I've been waiting for you to ask Me.' I replied that I did and He immediately began revealing the answers to my issues to me.

God created human beings with spirit, soul (the mind, emotions and will) and body, which are all knitted together and affect one another. When sin came in and separated us from God, who is our very source of life, we became self-centred. Our original, God-ordained, perfect personhood became distorted. That's why we struggle with so many problems and are often not even aware of the root causes of our issues – why we do what we do. The good news is that Jesus came to restore us in every area of personhood through the ministry of the Holy Spirit. By unwrapping every affected area with Him, the root causes of our issues will be revealed and then the truth in Christ can be restored, which will resolve our actual problems.

To show you how the ministry of the Holy Spirit functions, I will first explain how to apply His ministry in seven steps. Second, I will provide two examples of how this application has worked in my own life.

Holy Spirit Ministry

To follow the guidance of the Holy Spirit, you need to open all your spiritual senses to engage with Him. He can then guide and counsel you step by step. To do this, just keep watching and sensing what the Holy Spirit is showing you, keep listening to Jesus and keep communicating with Him.

1. **Choose a problem you want to deal with or choose a recent situation during which you experienced negative emotions, attitudes or behaviour.**

2. **Follow the Basic Ministry, given in Chapter 2, for repentance and forgiveness. Apply the Basic Ministry to the problem or situation you are dealing with (if relevant).**

3. **Ask the Holy Spirit to help you to explore your negative emotions or any physical conditions, such as tiredness or sickness, associated with this difficulty.** These are usually indicators that there are issues you need to deal with. Ask the Holy Spirit to help you to explore the thoughts and feelings that this particular problem has triggered. Be completely open and honest before Him. Describe your emotions as He reveals more and more. During this time, you might experience various moods, such as sadness, fear, anger, insecurity or anxiety. These

feelings may change as you dig deeper, moving from anger to fear or loneliness, for example.

4. **Ask the Holy Spirit to take you to the root of what He wants to deal with.** He will take you to the place where you first experienced the pain – a past event during which you accepted a wrong belief or a wrong perspective about yourself, God or others. Alternatively, He might take you to a place, an inner condition, that you might sense as being locked in a prison cell, for example.

5. **Ask the Holy Spirit to help you to explore the environment He's shown you, how you feel and what you're thinking.** (The Basic Ministry may be applied again, if relevant.) Focus on what He is showing you. Try not to use your own memory of the problem or event. We take on powerful wrong perspectives when we are hurt or suffer pain. These wrong perspectives continue to affect our lives long after the incident, a reality illustrated by people often saying something similar to 'Little me inside is reacting to certain situations.' During ministry, God is not changing your past but instead ministering to the 'present you' who is still affected by wrong perspectives. He wants to replace those perspectives with the truth. The deeper the examination of your emotions and thoughts, the deeper your healing. But God always respects your choice; He will not force you to do things that you don't want to do.

6. **Ask the Holy Spirit to help you to see where Jesus is, what He is doing, what He is saying and how you respond to Him. Do this until you are fully satisfied with the answers.** Jesus said, 'I am the way and the truth and the life' (John 14:6). So, if we want to see the true

perspective, we need to ask Him. Also, Jesus is everywhere (Jeremiah 23:23–24). So He must even be in the place you are exploring. Ask the Holy Spirit to help you to find Jesus. Once you meet Him, ask Jesus for the truth about each wrong perspective you have accepted and listen carefully for His response. As He talks with you, be honest and communicate until you fully understand and accept the truth He tells you. If you disagree or don't understand, tell Him. This process will sink deep into your core, becoming 'heart knowledge' as well as 'head knowledge'.

7. **Ask Jesus for tools to help you when you next face a similar situation.** Jesus will always give you tools that you can easily use. Again, don't take what He gives you if you can't apply them or agree to use them. Be honest with Him. Jesus said:

> Come to me, all you who are weary and burdened, and I will give you rest. Take my yoke upon you and learn from me, for I am gentle and humble in heart, and you will find rest for your souls. For my yoke is easy and my burden is light.
> (Matthew 11:28–30)

Example 1

1. Choose a problem you want to deal with or choose a recent situation in which you experienced negative emotions, attitudes or behaviour.

I felt jealous when someone was praised and loved by other people.

2. Basic Ministry.

'I repent of my jealousy and forgive myself for being jealous. I also choose to forgive the friends who didn't praise me and didn't express their love to me.'

3. Ask the Holy Spirit to help you to explore your negative emotions or any physical conditions, such as tiredness or sickness, associated with this difficulty.

I focus on feelings of jealousy. As I do so, the jealousy changes to anger and from anger to feeling abandoned, which then becomes a strong desire to have my friends' love.

4. Ask the Holy Spirit to take you to the root of what He wants to deal with.

I see myself at four years old. My newborn brother has just come home from hospital, and many people have come to visit him.

5. Ask the Holy Spirit to help you to explore the environment He's shown you, how you feel and what you're thinking.

(The Basic Ministry may be applied again, if relevant.)

The house is crowded and I am in a corner, outside a circle of people who are giving my baby brother all their attention. They are saying how gorgeous he is. I leave the corner and run around the room, trying to get some of their attention too, but nobody notices me. Suddenly, I trip and accidentally bump into the baby. He starts to cry and I am told off. I feel rejected and abandoned. I want to be comforted and loved too. I retreat to the corner crying, while everybody continues to adore my brother.

Basic Ministry: 'I choose to forgive my parents and relatives who didn't give me their attention. I even choose to forgive my brother who took all the attention, even though it wasn't his fault.'

6. Ask the Holy Spirit to help you to see where Jesus is, what He is doing, what He is saying and how you respond to Him.

Jesus is sitting in front of me, wiping away my tears.

JESUS: It's OK. I'm here. I love you.

I'm crying in His arms but start to feel better.

ME: Jesus, thank You, but I don't want Your love. You're not my parents. I want their love. Why can't I have it?
JESUS: They love you but they can't fully satisfy you.
ME: But I want their love. Jesus, let me try to get their love.

I continue trying to get my parents' love. Jesus is waiting behind me, holding a huge red heart. I am looking at them while Jesus is looking at me.

JESUS: Do you realize that I'm your parent?
ME: How?
JESUS: I made you. I love you and I always care for you. I have never left you and I'm the only one who can satisfy your hunger for love. I put you in the care of your parents, but I'm actually your creator.

This revelation brings me to tears.

ME: I didn't understand that before, but I do now. I'm sorry I've neglected You. You've been waiting for me. Thank You.

Jesus gives me the huge red heart He has been carrying. I know that I can bounce on it whenever I want to. He takes me to my parents so that I can receive their love too.

7. Ask Jesus for tools to help you when you next face a similar situation.

ME: Next time I feel jealous, what should I do?

JESUS: Remember My big heart is with you always. When you feel jealous, jump on it, like you'd bounce around on a trampoline, and enjoy it. Your jealousy will be gone. I love you, My daughter.

Testimony

I am now able to enjoy seeing other people receiving praise and love because I know that I am fully loved by Jesus.

Example 2

1. Choose a problem you want to deal with or choose a recent situation during which you experienced negative emotions, attitudes or behaviour.

I feel physically tired and irritated.

2. Basic Ministry.

Not applicable here.

3. Ask the Holy Spirit to help you to explore your negative emotions or any physical conditions, such as tiredness or sickness, associated with this difficulty.

As I focus on feeling tired and irritated, I start to feel sad, hopeless and even lonely. Tears are pouring down my face. I feel aimless and wander around.

4. Ask the Holy Spirit to take you to the root of what He wants to deal with.

I see myself as a hamster running in a wheel. It's quite dark and I'm alone. I can see the things I desire in front of me and I'm trying to get them.

5. Ask the Holy Spirit to help you to explore the environment He's shown you, how you feel and what you're thinking.

I feel as if I'm getting nowhere, chasing after the things I want, but if I stop, I won't get them either. I feel tired and want to stop, but fear is preventing me from doing so, although feelings of despair make me feel like giving up.

6. Ask the Holy Spirit to help you to see where Jesus is, what He is doing, what He is saying and how you respond to Him.

Jesus is standing next to me as I run in the wheel.

JESUS: Do you want to come down?
ME: Yes, but there are things I want to get and I need to try hard to get them.
JESUS: You may be able to get what you want but, as soon as you get it, you'll chase something else. It's a never-ending cycle.
ME: I still want to get these things, but I'll stop after that.
JESUS: OK. You go ahead.

Jesus waits for me while I continue trying to get what I want. At last, I manage it; I've got what I want. But then I spot something else even more appealing. I climb on to another wheel and start running again. Jesus continues to wait patiently. Finally, I stop.

ME: Jesus, You're right. The cravings for stuff are endless. I'll never be satisfied. But I haven't asked You for lots of things. I haven't been greedy. I just want a normal life. I gave up a lot of things for You and I feel miserable.

JESUS: When I was on earth, I didn't have any comfort. Remember, in Luke 9:58, I said that foxes have dens and birds of the air have nests, but the Son of Man has nowhere to lay His head? Why was this? It was all for your sake because I love you.

ME: That's true. I'm sorry I complain to You about my life when You sacrificed so much for me. I haven't even sacrificed all that much for You, yet I'm boasting about the little I've done. I said I would live for You but I forgot all about it.

JESUS: Life goes by so quickly. Focus on Me and walk with Me. I have prepared so many things for you. Remember to seek first God's Kingdom and His righteousness, and other things will be given to you as well [Matthew 6:33]. I have always provided for you, so there's no need to worry about what you need. I know what you need and what you want. I will take care of you. You just focus on Me and My Kingdom.

ME: OK, deal! Thank You for restoring my passion for You. Strangely, I don't crave those other things any more. Thank You.

Jesus leads me out of, and away from, the wheel. I start to see the beautiful field around it. It's so bright, with so many interesting things to do. I like it – there is so much freedom. Some people are building interesting things and I join them. Jesus watches what we're doing and smiles. This is what I've really longed for.

7. Ask Jesus for tools to help you when you next face a similar situation.

ME: Jesus, next time I start to chase things for my own comfort again, what shall I do? Are there any tools I can use?

JESUS: First, come to Me and see My smile. After this conversation, you will always remember what we have just talked about. This will help you to stop immediately and focus on My Kingdom and righteousness.

ME: When I start to chase after something, I may not be able to come to You. What shall I do?

JESUS: Every day, commit your day to Me and I will bless it. Just receive this – it's very simple. By doing this, you will be reminded each day that My face shines towards you. So don't chase after things but look at Me instead. Also, don't worry, I will always be faithful and bring you back, even if you forget or stray from Me.

Testimony

I have stopped looking for extra work to earn more to fulfil my need for comfort. Instead, I have started to use my free time to help at a charity. Rather than feeling tired and irritated, I feel much more joyful. A few months after this ministry with the Holy Spirit – and without any expectation or effort on my part – God provided me with extra regular income. Two years later I had saved enough for a deposit and was able to obtain a mortgage and buy a flat in

London. This was the first time I have ever had a home of my own. Indeed, God has proved His Word to me and He is still doing so: 'Seek first the kingdom of God and His righteousness, and all these things shall be added to you.' (Matthew 6:33 NKJV) Now, more of His Scriptures have become alive to me as I am further able to trust Him.

Go deeper

4

Further applications

Let's address some of our specific concerns by using the ministry of the Holy Spirit, which we explored in the previous chapter. As we apply this technique to deal with the different problems mentioned here, we will also learn how to deal with other issues affecting us now or that we might encounter in the future.

Addiction

Addiction may be defined as repeated, compulsive involvement with things, activities or, perhaps, people – even if they cause considerable harm – because that involvement brings pleasure or a sense of value. Examples can include overindulging in chocolate, food, alcohol, shopping, gaming, social media and exercise, or smoking, taking mind-altering substances (drugs), looking at pornography, pursuing a co-dependent (unhealthy) relationship, and so on.

How to address it:

1. Ask the Holy Spirit to reveal an addiction.
2. Basic Ministry: confess, repent, forgive and renounce, referring to the Basic Ministry guidelines in Chapter 2.

3. Apply the Holy Spirit Ministry method, referring to points 3 to 7 in Chapter 3.

  (a) Ask the Holy Spirit to reveal a root cause, starting event or cycle.

  (b) Ask the Holy Spirit to take you to the event and explore how you feel. Jesus is everywhere, so He must be there too. Sense where He is and what He is doing. Communicate honestly with Him until you fully agree with His truth.

  (c) Ask Him to give you the tools to use when tempted. Jesus will not condemn you; rather, He wants to walk with you on this journey. Even if you fail again and again, keep going back to Him because He can help you.

Example

1. Ask the Holy Spirit to reveal an addiction.
Masturbation.

2. Basic Ministry: confess, repent, forgive and renounce.

ME: I confess and repent of masturbation. I forgive myself for this act and for doing it so often. I renounce the pleasure of it and of fantasizing while doing it.

3. Apply the Holy Spirit Ministry method.

(a) Ask the Holy Spirit to reveal any root cause, starting event or cycle.

The Holy Spirit shows me that I masturbate when I feel empty and lonely. My first experience of this sensation was as a child, climbing up a metal pole when I was at primary school.

(b) Ask the Holy Spirit to take you to the event and explore how you feel. Jesus is everywhere, so He must be there too. Sense where He is and what He is doing. Communicate honestly with Him until you fully agree with His truth.

I see myself at the top of the metal pole, looking down. I'm lonely and missing my parents because they are at work. I suddenly experience a sensation and enjoy it. It gives me satisfaction and fills some of my emptiness, even though it's only short. I feel as though I need this and can't stop doing it. I feel that I'm now hooked by it and trapped in it. Jesus is sitting at the top of the pole next to me, while I'm hanging on. I want to hide from Him but I can see that He's not condemning me.

JESUS: I am with you. I like being with you. I'm the only one who can fill the emptiness inside you. What you feel through masturbation is only temporary and it's making you more miserable. Can you hand this over to Me?

For a while, I struggle to do so. I don't really want to let go of this pleasure. However, the more I hold on to it, the more miserable I feel. Finally, I'm able to hand this issue over to Jesus.

ME: Jesus, I feel guilty whenever I masturbate. I want to run away from You.

JESUS: Don't do that. I feel so sad when you run away. It hurts Me more than the wrong you've done. I will walk with you step by step and will never condemn you. I will cover you with My blood and cleanse you as white as snow. Come to Me now.

When I stretch my hands towards Jesus, I sense myself suddenly taken up to the sky, flying with Him. I feel so free and warm, secure and loved in His arms. I feel so comfortable and safe, and that I belong to Him. The air is filled with His love and it fills my empty heart. I feel so refreshed.

(c) Ask Him to give you the tools to use when tempted.

ME: Jesus, next time I'm longing to masturbate, what shall I do?

JESUS: Come to Me. You can fly high in My arms.

Testimony

After receiving ministry, my craving gradually disappeared as Jesus' love filled my heart.

Additional testimonies

Amelia: I was addicted to weed (marijuana). I couldn't stop smoking it, even though I knew it wasn't good for me. During ministry, Jesus took me back to a time when I was a little girl in my mother's house; she was also addicted to weed. I saw how I felt rejected and neglected by her but I still craved her attention very much. The smell of weed in the house was so familiar; I associated it with Mum and the craving for her love. I realized that was why I was addicted to weed. Jesus showed me how much He cares for me.

After I had ministry, I was free from my addiction to weed. I didn't crave it any more.

Harriet: I was addicted to TV. I knew I should stop watching it so much but I kept watching one show after another, even repeats. I would sacrifice sleep for it, and the following day I would always be so tired. During ministry, I sensed Jesus saying that He didn't condemn me. Rather, He enjoyed watching me enjoying TV, even though He didn't want me to be addicted to it. He asked me to watch it with Him. I also saw that I was quite lonely and was trying to fill that emptiness with TV.

Since receiving ministry, I've found it easier to stop because I watch TV with Jesus. Sometimes, I negotiate with Jesus whether I can watch one more episode. When I do, I'm able to stop watching after just that one. TV no longer traps me in the way that it did.

Accidents, shock and trauma

Accidents and trauma are deeply distressing, disturbing and stressful experiences. They cause emotional shock and injury that can lead to long-term negative effects on the soul – the mind, emotions and will – as well as on the body.

How to address them:

1. Ask the Holy Spirit to reveal a traumatic event in your life.
2. Basic Ministry: confess, repent, forgive and renounce.
3. Cut off any ungodly connection between you and the event/place/thing and break off the shock and trauma in Jesus' Name.
4. Apply the Holy Spirit Ministry method. Ask the Holy Spirit to take you to the event and explore how you feel. Jesus is everywhere, so He must be there too. Sense where He is and what He is doing. Communicate honestly with Him until you fully agree with His truth.
5. Pray for physical healing related to trauma, if necessary.
6. Reconnect and restore every part of your spirit, soul and body that is fractured and broken because of the shock and trauma.

Example

1. Ask the Holy Spirit to reveal a traumatic event in your life.

While I was having a driving lesson, I was involved in an accident. Another driver crashed into the side of my car because I didn't check my mirror when turning right. The other driver and I stopped and got out of our cars to check for damage to our vehicles. He said his car was fine and left, even though it was damaged.

2. Basic Ministry: confess, repent, forgive and renounce.

ME: I forgive myself for not looking in the mirror before manoeuvring. I confess and repent of believing that I'm stupid. I renounce all fear related to driving.

3. Cut off any ungodly connection between you and the event/place/thing and break off the shock and trauma in Jesus' Name.

ME: I cut off the ungodly connection between myself and the accident. I also break off the shock and trauma caused by this accident.

4. Apply the Holy Spirit Ministry method.

I feel very shaky and fearful and don't want to drive. I feel so bad; I think I'm stupid and should give up driving. Then, suddenly, I sense myself sitting on Jesus' lap, in a car, driving. He has His arm around me.

JESUS: Let's drive together. Don't worry, I'm protecting you. I know how to drive. You learn from Me. We'll look at the mirrors together.

I hesitate for a while but feel safe with Jesus. I start to enjoy learning how to drive and I don't feel fearful. I feel as if I'm driving in a big field. My fear has disappeared.

5. Pray for physical healing related to trauma, if necessary.

No physical healing is necessary.

6. Reconnect and restore every part of your spirit, soul and body that is fractured and broken because of the shock and trauma.

ME: Holy Spirit, I ask you to reconnect and restore every part of my spirit, soul and body to make me whole again.

Testimony

After ministry, I was able to take driving lessons again without feeling fearful and I eventually passed my test. Before ministry, the fear had been so strong that it felt as if it was gripping me. I thank God for His amazing healing.

Additional testimonies

Mia: I often got pins and needles, especially in the middle of the night. During ministry, the Holy Spirit took me back to a time when I was a toddler. I was with my mum at her workplace. I was enjoying being near my mum but, that day, a company inspector suddenly visited her department and I had to hide. My mum had to go out. She asked me to stay put, not to move and not to be caught, otherwise I would not be allowed to return to her workplace. I felt shock and trauma and didn't know what to do. I stayed hidden there and hardly moved until my mum came back.

During ministry, I started to get pins and needles; the sensation lasted for a long time. Jesus ministered to me. I was able to get rid of fear and receive a deep sense of freedom.

Since receiving ministry, I no longer get pins and needles in the middle of the night.

Tyler: I was afraid of getting into water because I nearly drowned at a swimming pool when I was a kid. During ministry, I saw myself being thrown into the pool by my uncle, who was taking care of me. He knew I couldn't swim but he said the best way to learn was to be thrown in at the deep end. I was drowning and drank lots of water. When I was rescued, I was crying really hard. I hated my uncle and never wanted to go near a swimming pool or deep water ever again. Even though I had tried to conquer my fear of deep water by having swimming lessons, the fear remained.

I forgave my uncle and saw Jesus rescuing me and protecting me. My fear lifted and I am much more confident now. Following ministry, I was able to appreciate the beauty of water and swimming.

An orphan heart

People with orphan hearts are people who have emotionally (if not physically) 'left home'. They search everywhere continually for acceptance and belonging. They have no safe place to go in their hearts, minds or emotions. Like the prodigal son, they wander from place to place, always searching, and yet never finding anywhere they feel valued or affirmed for who they are. Alternatively, they begin to strive to achieve and perform at a high level for affirmation and love, especially from parents or other authority figures.

This ministry will help those with orphan hearts to know and believe that they are truly sons and daughters of our loving heavenly Father.

How to address it:

1. Ask the Holy Spirit to show you when you acquired an orphan heart or when you emotionally 'left home'.
2. Basic Ministry: confess, repent, forgive and renounce.
3. Apply the Holy Spirit Ministry method. Ask the Holy Spirit to take you to the event and explore how you feel. Jesus is everywhere, so He must be there too. Sense where He is and what He is doing. Communicate honestly with Him until you fully agree with His truth.
4. Ask Jesus to take you to God your Father to see how you relate to Him. If you experience any difficulties, express what's in your heart and listen to what He says. Do this until you fully agree with His truth.
5. Take time to receive His love. Don't rush away; enjoy that time with Him.

Example

1. Ask the Holy Spirit to show you when you acquired an orphan heart or when you emotionally 'left home'.

The Holy Spirit showed me that, emotionally, I left home when I was in secondary school. I thought my parents were too controlling and I wanted to run away from them. As a result, I always tip-toed around people because it didn't feel safe to be myself around them.

I can see now why I feel too tired and stressed to relate to others.

2. Basic Ministry: confess, repent, forgive and renounce.

ME: I choose to forgive my parents for controlling me, for nagging me to study and for making me feel as though I didn't have any freedom. I confess and repent of my rebellion against my parents, leaving home in my heart and becoming emotionally detached. I renounce the slave mentality that made me feel controlled.

3. Apply the Holy Spirit Ministry method.

I see myself running away from my parents' control but then getting hurt by others because I feel unprotected. There's a lot of pain in my heart; I'm fearful and looking around. I feel quite cold but I don't want to go back home; I don't want to be controlled. I don't like being at home or away from home.

Jesus asks me to come to Him. He is shining brightly and looks warm, but I don't want to go to Him because I worry that He is going to control me too. I can see that I'm being stubborn. I try to enjoy my freedom for a while, despite the dangers around me. As time goes by, I feel pain and emptiness inside. But Jesus is still here.

JESUS: I'm still waiting for you. I don't control you and, if you think that I'm controlling you, you can go again.

I carefully approach. I start to feel at home, feeling warmth and belonging. I wonder why I ran away for so long because I obviously belong here. Jesus shows me how my parents loved me and tried to protect me.

4. Ask Jesus to take you to God your Father to see how you relate to Him.

Jesus takes me to God the Father. He is very big and I hesitate to go to Him. I stand behind Jesus instead. With His big arms open, God the Father asks me to come and Jesus encourages me to go. I look at God the Father's face – He has a big smile. I have never seen that before. It's really dazzling. I know deep inside that He loves me. God the Father hugs Jesus and I follow Him so that I can be a part of the embrace too. It's an amazing feeling. God the Father says, 'I love you, My daughter, welcome home.' I feel a continual overflowing of love.

5. Take time to receive His love.

I keep receiving His love until it fills me to overflowing.

Testimony

Since receiving ministry, I feel more comfortable with being myself. I don't worry about what other people think of me as much. I can even express my negative feelings without being ashamed. I can be who I am.

Additional testimonies

Dewey: During ministry, the Holy Spirit showed me how, as a boy between the ages of ten and eighteen, I tried to gain acceptance and love from my parents. In particular, I felt I had to earn or win my father's love and approval. I couldn't say no to anyone. The Holy Spirit reminded me of my nickname, 'Skinny', meaning weak. He showed me the root of the problem, taking me back to the time when my parents had come over to the UK but had left me behind in Singapore. I was crying under my wooden bed. It was dark, I felt lonely and that nobody cared for or loved me. I felt weak, ugly and hopeless. The Holy Spirit showed me that I acquired an orphan heart that day.

From underneath the bed, I saw Jesus' legs and feet but I was too weak to come out. I couldn't face seeing Jesus. Eventually, He bent down, picked me up and hugged me. He gave me a piggyback and started to run around. That really cheered me up and I started giggling. He asked me to hold on to Him and I felt secure. I didn't feel the need to win or earn anything. Instead, it was OK just to be myself. Jesus showed me a rainbow and told me that's how He sees me too – beautiful, useful and loved. I also saw an ugly duckling, representing me. Later, this duckling turned into a beautiful swan. Then, Jesus took me to Father God and I played chess with Him, then hide and seek. I had so much fun. While spending time with God, I was free to be myself. I lay down on His lap for a while, receiving His love as I slept, and woke up feeling refreshed. I now understand that God loves me no matter what and He will never abandon me.

Since receiving this ministry, I have been able to say no to things and people. I don't need to earn their acceptance or win their love. I don't feel scared or fearful that they might not like me. I feel more at home with God and feel comfortable whenever I think of Him, and even when I face challenging issues.

Bella: When I was four, my younger brother developed polio and nearly died. During that time, my mother's focus was entirely on him. Many times, I was left on my own outside doctors' surgeries and shops, while my mother and brother were inside. During ministry, the Holy Spirit showed me that, because I felt excluded, my feelings began to shut down. This continued until I was eight, when an incident occurred that was the last straw for me; emotionally, I left home and made myself an orphan. I realize now that my hope for a better relationship with my mother had died. I had long since given up on my absentee father. So, growing up, my image of God was distorted. I believed He was someone who was always remote, far away, busy – too busy for me. He was never there when I needed Him and was very strict, an angry bully. I had a relationship with Jesus but I felt disconnected from my heavenly Father because I carried an orphan heart.

Jesus took me by the hand – I felt like a young child again – and said, 'It's time for you to meet your heavenly Father.' We went into a room in a house. In the next room, there was a big golden light at the far end. I let go of Jesus' hand and ran as fast as my little legs would carry me. I jumped up into the light, as if I were jumping on to an adult's lap. It's hard to describe the feeling of peace, joy, love, warmth and contentment – the sheer bliss and relief – that washed over me and enveloped me. At last I was home. I felt so safe in His presence, which enabled me to open the door to my poor numb emotions and let them out. Rage and grief poured out of me like lava from a volcano. I shocked myself. I had no idea so much was locked deep inside me. Then, when the volcanic eruption had subsided, Jesus showed me my parents again and I saw them through His eyes. I was filled with compassion and understanding for them, for their suffering and how wounded they were. I was able to forgive them.

So, after I found my home in my heavenly Father, Jesus restored my relationship with my earthly parents, healed my image of fatherhood and of God, and set me completely free from my orphan heart.

Rejection

When we believe we are rejected or dismissed as inadequate, we search for acceptance or try to protect ourselves from being rejected again by rejecting others. A common problem associated with rejection is self-rejection or self-hatred.

How to address it:

1. Ask the Holy Spirit to show you when you first believed that you were rejected.
2. Basic Ministry: confess, repent, forgive and renounce.
3. Apply the Holy Spirit Ministry method. Ask the Holy Spirit to take you to the event and explore how you feel. Jesus is everywhere, so He must be there too. Sense where He is and what He is doing. Communicate honestly with Him until you fully agree with His truth.
4. Accept and love yourself.
5. Soak in the love of God.

Example

1. Ask the Holy Spirit to show you when you first felt rejected.

I was in my mother's womb. My grandma wanted my mother to have a boy rather than a girl, so I felt rejected from that moment. While growing up, I worked to make myself acceptable by studying hard and trying to be a good daughter. Now, I can't say no to people and I keep trying to please them.

2. Basic Ministry: confess, repent, forgive and renounce.

ME: I forgive my grandma for preferring boys to girls and for letting me believe that I wasn't good enough to be alive in this world. I confess, repent of and renounce believing that boys are more important than girls, and that I'm rejected. I confess and repent of blaming God for making me a girl.

3. Apply the Holy Spirit Ministry method.

I see myself in my mother's womb. It's small and I'm in a corner, crouching in the dark, feeling abandoned and rejected.

I feel as if darkness is hiding me. Despite the negative feelings, it's comfortable in that position and I don't want to come out into the world but light starts to invade. I move further back, away from the light. I don't want to show myself. Then Jesus covers me with a silky blanket – He is there with me. I feel safe and there is light. He looks at me, smiling, and says, 'Do you know I made you? You're beautiful!' But I am upset and angry.

ME: Why didn't You make me a boy? I'm not important. I'm not wanted. I don't like it. I don't like You for making me a girl.

JESUS: So, you don't like what I made? That makes Me sad. I really like you as you are.

I feel bad that I complained.

ME: Sorry, Jesus, but my grandma wanted a boy. My culture likes boys. Where is my place?

JESUS: Look at Me. I really like you as you are and I think I made you very well. You're in My heart.

He picks me up, puts me on His shoulders and starts to walk along the road. He announces loudly to people, 'This is my daughter. I'm so proud of her.'

I suddenly start to see how Jesus sees me: adorable, lovely and precious. I feel so loved by Him. Nothing can take His love away from me. I realize that I've rejected myself. I burst into tears and cry loudly. I have rejected this beautiful girl God made.

4. Accept and love yourself.

I apologize to myself for my self-rejection. I give myself a big hug; I accept myself and release all the love I've held back all those years. I feel so loved.

5. Soak in the love of God.

I sense Jesus hugging me. I continue to receive His love until it overflows.

Testimony

Since receiving ministry, I've begun to like myself. When I look at myself in the mirror, I see a beautiful person. Before ministry, whenever I looked in the mirror, I saw someone ugly. Now, I can also say no without fear of rejection. I feel so free.

Additional testimonies

Scarlett: In my family, people always like to compare siblings and show favouritism. I have a half-sister and, because a lot of my relatives were fearful of her mother (my stepmum), they praised my half-sister all the time, saying that she was so cute, so clever, and so on. The worst part of it was that they would compare me with her. I often felt angry, jealous, hurt, undermined and unimportant. Even my own father called me by my half-sister's nickname. He couldn't be bothered to correct it; I felt so rejected. My dad liked to share jokes with her but, when it came to me, we talked about work most of the time. He would praise her in front of me and I wondered whether he loved her more than me.

During ministry, I exchanged the lies I had believed for the truth. After ministry, I was able to love my dad and my sister because I had discovered my identity in Christ. During a family gathering at which my sister and I were present, some relatives immediately focused on her and praised her looks. I just stood by, smiled and thought to myself, 'I'm beautiful too.' I didn't need them to tell me so because I knew who

I was (and who I am) – the daughter of the Most High. I said to myself, 'I am royalty, a princess.' Because I understood who I truly was, I no longer felt rejected at all. I was able to agree with our relatives and say, 'Yes, she is beautiful. Look at her!'

Layla: From a very young age, I had to do all the chores at home and, because my family was very poor, I also went out to work. I got married early so that I could escape the heavy responsibility I had at home. However, during all those years of marriage, my husband demanded that I work and work and work. I felt guilty when I had a moment's rest. I believed that no one cared for me and that I was a slave and a machine. I felt so rejected.

During ministry, I saw how precious I am to Jesus. I saw that I am a warrior princess, not a slave. I no longer think that I have to be perfect to be valued, and I don't have to work hard to obtain people's love. Since receiving ministry, I have been able to enjoy resting without feeling guilty. I've also learned to treat myself to good things.

Ungodly beliefs

Ungodly beliefs take root when we accept the lies the enemy tells us about God, the world and ourselves. These lies then determine how we perceive our lives.

How to address them:

1. Ask the Holy Spirit to show you your ungodly belief and an event related to it.
2. Basic Ministry: confess, repent, forgive and renounce.
3. Apply the Holy Spirit Ministry method. If the Holy Spirit shows you a specific event, ask to be taken to it and explore how you feel. Jesus is everywhere, so He must

be there too. Sense where He is and what He is doing. Communicate honestly with Him until you fully agree with His truth.

4. If no specific event is recalled, ask God to show you the truth in contrast to all the lies. Be honest and ask questions until you fully agree with His truth.
5. Ask if there are any other tools you could use.
6. Receive the truth about yourself in your spirit.

Example

1. Ask the Holy Spirit to show you your ungodly belief and an event related to it.

I believe that my opinion is not important. I was good at debating at school and I always won debates in my high-school class. But one day, I was telling my dad what I thought about school and he suddenly became upset. He told me I was wrong and he didn't want to listen to me.

From that time, I became fearful of expressing my opinions to him and, later, to others too. Also, I often found that people wouldn't listen to me when I suggested ideas. Even though my ideas were similar to other people's, mine always seemed to be rejected. Because of these things, I believed that there was no point in expressing my opinion.

2. Basic Ministry: confess, repent, forgive and renounce.

I choose to forgive my dad, who refused to listen to my opinions. I confess, repent of and renounce the ungodly belief that my opinion is not good enough and that it's not important.

3. Apply the Holy Spirit Ministry method.

I see myself in my parents' room, talking to my dad. I'm stunned by his sudden anger. It's as if a big metal wall has come down in front of me. I feel shocked and trapped behind it. Whatever I say, I can't be heard. Even if I shout, it's as if nobody can hear me. I bang on the wall to escape but I can't. I become frustrated and angry; my anger is like a volcano that keeps erupting. I'm swearing – I've never sworn at anyone before, even myself. I'm shocked. It takes such a long time to stop that volcanic eruption.

But the volcano can't break down the wall either. It is so thick, and it's icy cold too. I'm exhausted and feel hopeless. Jesus is sitting on top of the wall, very high up. I don't think there is any point in shouting for help because Jesus won't hear. I sigh.

JESUS: Why are you sighing?
ME: Can you hear my sigh from that far up?
JESUS: [*smiling*] Of course. I heard your swearing too.

He comes down from the wall and sits with me.

JESUS: Talk to Me. I'm interested in what you have to say. I love to hear your voice.
ME: People don't listen to me. Even my dad refused to listen to my opinions.
JESUS: Your dad was upset that day after a hard time at work. Do you remember that he was a headmaster who had responsibility for managing the whole school? That day, some people had complained to him about the school. He wasn't really upset with you; he was just stressed by his problems at work. Anyway, I love to hear your opinions and I love reasoning with you. It's fascinating hearing what you have to say.
ME: How can You be fascinated when You know everything?

JESUS: You know how you love to hear and watch toddlers? What they say fascinates you, even though you know more than they do. That's how I feel towards you. You give Me joy when you talk and reason with Me. If you knew how I felt, you wouldn't ask these questions. Now, shall we leave this place?

ME: We can't, the wall is too thick. Can You help?'

JESUS: You're the one who has closed yourself in, not others, because you want to protect yourself. You just need to open the door.

I notice a door in the wall and wonder how to open it. Suddenly, I see buttons all over the wall and I choose one to press. It opens a small door. I press another and it opens another round door. I press lots of buttons. They open different doors and I see bright light outside. I feel hesitant about going out because I'm still fearful, so I look at Jesus. He smiles and takes my hand. I feel safer and slowly walk out. The light is so bright and pleasant; I can see flowers, trees and people playing. Jesus greets them and they greet Him. They smile and wave to me too. I feel secure and recognized because I am with Jesus.

4. If no specific event is recalled, ask God to show you the truth in contrast to all the lies.

Not relevant.

5. Ask if there are any other tools you could use.

Jesus gives me a tool – whenever I think that people aren't listening to me or that my opinion isn't important, I should look at Him. When I do, He says, 'I'm listening to you,' and I see Him leaning down, His ear turned towards me to hear me speak. His ear becomes huge to catch my every word.

6. Receive the truth about yourself in your spirit.

ME: Jesus, I receive the truth in my spirit that my opinions
        are important to You. You are always listening to me,
        even my smallest sigh. You like to hear my voice.

I receive assurance from Him because of this truth, especially
from the image of His huge ear listening to me.

Testimony

After receiving ministry, I became able to express my opinions
and, surprisingly, people now listen to me and agree with
what I say. They even seem to like my ideas. Even when
people sometimes ignore what I say, it doesn't matter any
more. Jesus is still listening to me with His huge ear.

Additional testimonies

Isla: I used to think of myself as fat and ugly. I wished I could
have a slim body and not have to worry about dieting. I
wished I could have bigger eyes too. I failed at every diet and
wanted to have plastic surgery. During ministry, Jesus showed
me that I was trying to conform to worldly standards. He
reminded me of a time when someone commented that my
eyes were pretty; I got upset and angry because I thought he
was mocking me. The truth was that this person really did
like my eyes. Jesus also showed me that I shouldn't focus on
what to eat and I shouldn't worry about putting on weight;
instead, I should be grateful for what I ate and enjoy it. He
wanted me to be healthy and not to focus on my weight.
Eventually, I would have a healthy weight.

After ministry, I began to see myself through Jesus' eyes.
I even started to like my own small eyes. I applied Jesus'
advice about thanking God for the food that I ate and

enjoying it rather than worrying about my weight. Without dieting, I managed to lose weight that, before, I hadn't been able to shed while trying all kinds of expensive diets. I'm no longer as bothered about my looks as I used to be.

Jasper: Whenever something I was doing didn't go right, I would become agitated and angry with myself. Tiny things, such as dropping a hanger, could set me off and I would have to repeat the task. While agitated, I would find myself cursing and swearing, telling myself that I was stupid, useless, an idiot and that I couldn't even get this small task right. Most of the time, when something like that happened, this tape of criticism would play in my head.

During ministry, the Holy Spirit took me back to a time when I had just started school. It was Christmas, there was a present under the bed and I would soon be getting up to go to church. Lying on the bed, my eyes still shut, I overheard my dad telling my mum that I was stupid and useless. This was because, that first year in school, my results weren't good. Even the teacher seemed surprised. Also, to make things worse, a family friend had come to the house the previous day and had compared my results with his son's, who had done better than I had.

I heard Jesus saying, 'I am with you, bearing your hurts and fears. Don't be afraid; I am with you. You're not useless; I am with you. Hear from Me.' The fear of my dad's being angry had also bred insecurity; a fear that, if I didn't do well at school, he wouldn't value or love me. So, I had grown up feeling insecure and attempted to deal with it by doing well. During most of my school life, except the last year, I made sure I did well enough and I received a lot of presents from my parents.

I asked Jesus about the fact that I had problems with outbursts and swearing whenever something didn't turn out right. He said, 'Just say "Yo!"' I had to laugh at that. I thought it was so weird. It's not a word I use. But among other things, this word is used for getting someone's attention: 'Hear me'. I thought that was amazing – wasn't that what the Lord had told me earlier? 'Hear from Me!' It told of a close relationship.

Following ministry, a test came when I was packing a box. Halfway through, and thinking I'd packed it well so far, I flipped it over, only to hear a moving sound. Ordinarily, this would have got me worked up but, this time, I remained calm. Also, immediately after ministry, the frequency of my swearing went down so much that I rarely swear now.

Inner vows

Inner vows are very similar to ungodly beliefs, except that they are far stronger because we use our willpower to make sure that we act on them. An inner vow is a determination, statement or directive that will make our hearts, minds or lives go a certain way. Our vows determine how our lives are to be lived, causing us to create set structures or patterns.

How to address them:

1. Ask the Holy Spirit to show you any hidden inner vows you have made and any events related to them.
2. Basic Ministry: confess, repent, forgive and renounce.
3. Apply the Holy Spirit Ministry method. If the Holy Spirit shows you a specific event, ask to be taken to it and explore how you feel. Jesus is everywhere, so He must be there too. Sense where He is and what He is doing. Communicate honestly with Him until you fully agree with His truth.
4. Ask Jesus what He is going to give you in exchange for breaking this inner vow.
5. Ask if there are any other tools you could use.

Example

1. Ask the Holy Spirit to show you any hidden inner vows you have made and any events related to them.

I've told myself that I'm clumsy. The Holy Spirit showed me that this vow came from my belief that I had failed in my responsibility as an eldest daughter; I saw my primary-school-aged sister have an accident that I couldn't prevent.

2. Basic Ministry: confess, repent, forgive and renounce.

ME: I confess that I agreed with the enemy's lies that I am clumsy and accident-prone, and that it's better for me to be hurt than my siblings. I repent of agreeing with these lies. I renounce and break off my inner vow in Jesus' Name. I forgive myself for not caring for myself.

3. Apply the Holy Spirit Ministry method.

I see my sister running across the pedestrian crossing ahead of me. I'm busy eating a snack. There is a crowd in the middle of the road and I see my sister on the ground. She has been knocked down by a car. I'm shocked and I don't know what to do. We are taken to hospital by the driver involved in the accident. That evening, my mum is crying for my sister. Afterwards, I have to take care of my sister because she has difficulty walking for a month. I feel guilty that I couldn't protect her. I believe that I should have suffered instead of her and that I have let my parents down. I feel it would be better for me to get hurt instead of my sister or brother. I want to protect and take care of my siblings and I don't care about myself.

I see myself trying to protect them but I continually get hurt. Despite my best efforts, they aren't fully protected anyway. It's such a heavy responsibility. I want to run away but I can't or they might get hurt even more. I feel as though I'm being buffeted again and again by strong winds. I'm very vulnerable.

Suddenly, Jesus calms the wind. I flop down on the ground feeling very exhausted.

JESUS: Will you allow Me to help you?
ME: I'm afraid my siblings will get hurt. I try so hard to protect them but I can't.
JESUS: Can you hand them over to Me? I'll protect them.

Eventually, I give them to Jesus. I can see they are in safe hands and are well protected. It's such a relief and I thank Him.

JESUS: Don't you want Me to protect you and keep you safe too?

I suddenly realize how badly I have treated myself. I believe that I have the power to protect either my siblings or myself but not all of us, so I need to sacrifice myself if I want to protect them. So I've left myself unprotected and I haven't cared for myself.

ME: Can I come to You? Can I be protected too?
JESUS: Of course. I want to protect you too. You have suffered a lot. It's very painful to see My girl neglecting herself. Do you know how precious you are to Me? You are My daughter and princess, someone who needs to be well cared for.

I can see that Jesus cares for me as if He's holding the most precious thing.

ME: Yes, I'd like that. I'm sorry for not caring for myself so far. Thank You for caring for me and protecting me. I will treat myself better.

4. Ask Jesus what He is going to give you in exchange for breaking this inner vow.

I sense Jesus giving me a beautiful glossy white dress. He tells me to put it on and walk with Him. I walk with Him carefully and elegantly because I don't want to damage it but, strangely, I feel so free in it, as if it were my usual comfortable clothing.

5. Ask if there are any other tools to use.

JESUS: Remember, you should always wear this white dress. It will remind you who you are in Me and how you should treat yourself.

Testimony

After ministry, I started to care for myself. I began to see how precious I am; I now sense that I'm wearing the white dress Jesus gave me. Before ministry, if I hurt myself, I didn't pay much attention. For me, it was just another bump or bruise. But now I take time to care for myself, and I'm more careful about not injuring myself.

Additional testimonies

Elsie: I was abused by a youth club leader when I was a teenager. So, to protect myself, I vowed that I would never grow up to be a woman. After all, if such a thing had happened to me as a teenager, how much more abuse would I face as an adult? Even though I was growing physically, I tried to remain like a child and avoid facing reality. People treated me like a child too. I hated the idea of getting older.

During ministry, I received Jesus' assurance that He would always be with me and protect me, even though I was growing up. Jesus also showed me how important and how cool it is to be an adult.

After ministry, I started to mature into the person I am now. People respect me and even come to me for advice.

Roman: One of my inner vows was, 'I will be alone at the end because I was rejected by my spouse.'

During ministry, God showed me how I got stranded and lost in a big city without any money when I was a young boy. As I was walking, I saw Jesus walking with me, guiding me back home. He said that He would never leave me and would always be with me. He also told me that I have His gift for connecting people for His kingdom.

Since receiving ministry, I can see how much I am loved by God and by people. I fully know that God gave me a good life to enjoy and people around me who love me very much. I am now actively fulfilling God's purpose by connecting people to one another.

A hardened heart

If we don't feel safe in certain environments, we learn to protect ourselves. Our basic ability to trust is challenged and our hearts begin to close. When we make the choice to close off part of our hearts, we put up walls around them. We will not be able to receive love, even though we might be able to give it. We might not even be able to see the beauty around us, in the things that God has created.

How to address it:

1. Ask the Holy Spirit to show you the state of your heart.
2. Ask Him where the root of this state of the heart lies and to reveal any experiences or events to which you responded by shutting down or building walls.
3. Basic Ministry: confess, repent, forgive and renounce.
4. Apply the Holy Spirit Ministry. Ask God to take you to the root of your situation and explore how you feel. Jesus is everywhere, so He must be there too. Sense where He is and what He is doing. Communicate honestly with Him until you fully agree with His truth.
5. Ask the Holy Spirit to reveal the state of your heart again. See if there is any change. If not, ask Him to change it for you.
6. If there is still no change, ask Him if there is anyone you need to forgive, anything you need to do or any lies you believe that you need to address.

Example

1. Ask the Holy Spirit to show you the state of your heart.

I sense that half my heart is made of metal and the other half is made of flesh.

2. Ask Him where the root of this state of the heart lies.

I had a boyfriend at school whom I liked a lot. When my parents found out, they were very displeased and, because I was so afraid of them, I ended the relationship. While saying goodbye, my boyfriend told me he was bored with me, despite the fact that I'd done all I could to treat him well. It was a huge shock. I thought I was offering the most sacrificial love but he just thought I was boring. After that, I thought that people wouldn't like me if I poured out my love and opened up to them. I stopped trusting others. Later, I had another boyfriend and we wanted to get married. He met my parents and we arranged the wedding. But, suddenly, after meeting his mentor, he turned sour. He told me that he couldn't marry me even though God had told him to get married. It was another huge shock. Again, I accepted the lie that people didn't like me when I got close to them. I built walls around my heart.

3. Basic Ministry: confess, repent, forgive and renounce.

ME: I confess to believing the lie that people won't like me when I get close to them. I repent of believing this lie. I repent of and renounce putting up walls to protect myself. I forgive those two boyfriends who rejected me when I gave all my love to them.

4. Apply the Holy Spirit Ministry method.

I see myself trying to hide a box. I believe that people won't like me or will even abandon me if they see inside it. I believe I will be safe as long as no one opens it. I guard it closely. I put all my attention and energy into hiding it. Jesus walks towards me with a smile.

JESUS: What are you doing? Shall we have some fun together?

I agree that we should and I enjoy my time with Him. But my attention is still on that box in case He or anyone else opens it. I keep watching the box and Jesus keeps looking at me. I feel bad about not being able to give Him my full attention.

ME: Sorry, Jesus. I need to guard the box. I'm sorry I can't spend time with You properly.

JESUS: May I guard the box for you?

ME: That's fine. I don't want You to see inside the box.

JESUS: Why? I already know what's inside and I like it.

ME: No, Jesus, You don't. I can't believe You like what's inside.

JESUS: Yes, I do. In fact, I think you'll like it too.

ME: No way! I've been hiding it for so long because people leave me when they see what's inside it.

JESUS: Why are you hiding something I like so much? Show Me what's inside the box.

ME: If I do that, I'm afraid You'll leave me too, and that will make me so sad.

JESUS: I promise I will never leave you. Shall we look at it together?

With some hesitation, I reluctantly let Jesus open the box. But fear grips me and I'm afraid to look at it. Suddenly, I smell a nice fragrance coming from the box. Jesus is enjoying looking in the box and smelling the fragrance. Slowly, I approach Jesus and look at the open box. There are flowers inside and, when I look more closely, I can see a big red heart-shaped crystal producing them. What a relief! I thought there were only dirty, horrible things in there. I am so tearful.

JESUS: Look at how beautiful the flowers are. Try touching this heart. Even though it's crystal, it's so soft.

Jesus kisses the heart and it becomes bigger, like a sponge soaked in water. More flowers grow. Jesus gives me the heart to hold. It feels so strange – it's shiny crystal but soft, like a teddy bear. The smell of flowers is so strong.

JESUS: It's your heart. It's well protected by Me, like hard crystal, but it's also soft when you open up to people, showing them who you really are. You can receive more of My love as you become who you are. Don't hide it.

He asks whether we should throw the box away. I agree that we should. I don't need it any more. I hid the contents for so long but they are beautiful. I'm grateful to Jesus for showing me what was inside the box. I was so fearful but now I feel free.

ME: What should I do if people don't like me or leave me, like my previous boyfriends, when I open up to them?

JESUS: Remember who you are. You bless people and spread My fragrance. Some people may not value your love but it's their loss, not yours. I love your heart. I enjoy you; I never get bored with you and I want to be with you. I will be with you always.

5. Ask the Holy Spirit to show you the state of your heart again.

I sense the metal part of my heart has changed to red, soft crystal.

6. If there is still no change, ask Him if there is anyone you need to forgive, anything you need to do or any lies you believe that you need to address.

Not relevant.

Testimony

Since receiving ministry, I've felt safe enough to open my heart and receive love from other people. I didn't before, even though people expressed love and praise to me; I didn't believe that they meant it. I'm grateful to have many friends who love me as I am.

Additional testimonies

Niamh: My heart was very hard because I lived in lots of different homes when I was young. I felt that no one would ever care for me. I just needed to survive. A symptom of my hard heart was that I didn't understand how people could enjoy nature. To me, it just seemed like wasting time.

During ministry, Jesus showed me how He had always cared for me and how He had sent others to care for me too.

After ministry, my perspective on my past changed completely. I started to notice how flowers are all very different, and how lovely and fascinating butterflies are. God cares for each one so beautifully and wonderfully, as He does for me. My life has become fuller now; I can enjoy people and the things around me.

Summer: I thought I'd found the man who would be my husband. When we didn't marry, I felt disappointed and hardened my heart. I saw what it looked like – soft on the outside with a hard shell on the inside.

I asked God to show me the root cause of the state of my heart. A time came to mind when I was in the school playground, aged about nine, waiting for my mum to pick me up at the end of the day. I was feeling alone; I was the last child to be picked up and I was wondering why my mum was late. I looked at the cars coming down the road, searching for hers. I felt impatient. I sensed that Jesus was in the playground near me, looking at me. I wondered why I was impatient. What was I missing at home while I was waiting?

I had a revelation that I wasn't missing out on anything. I was fine waiting; Jesus was there. I felt comfortable and able to wait. What is my heart like now? The hard shell on the inside has become soft, like jelly.

Stay in

5

Keep walking with God

When you receive the truth that God gives you, Satan wants to reinforce his lies by taking it away. He will keep trying to feed you lies, using different people and situations, but if you resist his attempts, he will leave you alone (James 4:7). Hold on to God's truth.

Here is one of many testimonies about how Satan tries to rob us of the truth about ourselves:

> Just after I'd received ministry for my long-standing belief that I was not important, my brother told me, 'You're not important.' The next day, my best friend said the same thing. It felt so strange and upsetting. It never used to bother me when people said that because I'd believed it my whole life anyway. But now that I knew I truly was important, it upset me. Immediately, I asked God, 'What do You say about that?' He reminded me again that I am precious and important to Him. I sensed Him starting to stroke my head, which helped me to understand how much He felt for me: that I was so dear and so precious. Now, I'm more confident about how important I am to Him, even when people say negative things about me.

As this example shows, when we go to God, He will reaffirm the truth; He will reinforce it at deeper levels in our hearts.

The trouble is that the world around us can distract and draw us away again. Let's imagine you're singing 'Twinkle, twinkle, little star' but a crowd facing you is singing 'London Bridge is falling down'. You'll find it very difficult to continue singing your song without becoming distracted and eventually singing the other tune instead. However, if someone assists you by singing your song into your ear, and blocking out the song from the crowd by placing a hand over your other ear, you'll be able to continue singing without being distracted.

God is here to sing the truth into your heart. Can you hear His voice? Can you continue to sing the truth of how precious you are to Him? You can only do this when you focus on His voice. Focus on the truth God has spoken to you. Don't bother about what the world says concerning you and God.

Each year, for several years now, I have been receiving ministry from the Holy Spirit for more than twenty different issues. For me, negative emotions, attitudes and behaviour are indications that I need to deal with deeper conditions. I bring things to God every time He nudges me. Whenever He deals with something, I receive His truth and grow closer to Him. As a result, I have tasted increased, abundant life. Sometimes, He deals with certain problems in greater depth; at other times, He deals with several wider issues. Either way, I grow every time I bring them to Him, and I find it very exciting each time I deal with them. I hope that you will make recognizing God's nudges and immediately going to Him part of your lifestyle too.

To help you to understand how the healing or sanctification process can work, the following pages contain two illustrations of the steps involved.

Frothy Water Bottle

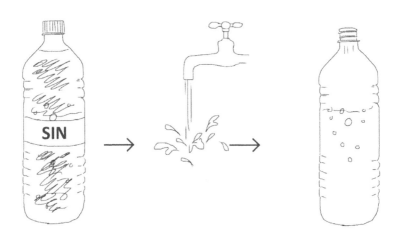

(a) The label is peeled off the bottle and its lid is opened.
By repenting of your sins, accepting Jesus Christ as your Lord and Saviour, and opening your heart to the Holy Spirit, your sin is removed as Jesus becomes your righteousness.

(b) There is frothy water in the bottle.
You still have baggage, hurts and problems from the past that have to be addressed over time.

(c) Clean, still water pours in from the tap.
The Holy Spirit starts to work in you – sanctification begins.

(d) Some of the frothy water pours out.

This is when ministry is received to deal with, and cleanse you from, past baggage, hurts or problems.

(e) Some bubbles still remain.

You still have some unresolved issues.

(f) More bubbles enter the bottle unless it is continually filled with clean, still water.
You can be affected by additional issues because of the influence of the world around you, unless you're continually filled with the Spirit.

(g) More bubbles surface as clean, still water is poured in.
Problems keep surfacing. This is a good thing! God is dealing with you and you are growing in Him. A mountain looks beautiful from afar but, when you reach it, you see all the waste left by people and animals. The closer you are to Jesus, the more you will see your own dirt. But God is holy and will deal with your problems when you are ready. God wants you to have abundant life. You're in the process of walking into it. When you are filled with the Holy Spirit, He will lead you in the right direction, even during your Scriptural meditation. You will have increased desire and understanding of the Word of God.

Sticky Notes Versus Cloths

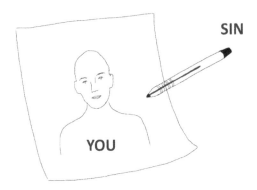

(a) Paper with lots of dots drawn on it.
This demonstrates the fact that human beings have committed lots of sins. We can't remove them by ourselves.

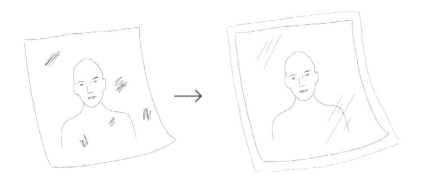

(b) Clean, laminated paper.
When you repent of your sins and accept Jesus Christ as your Saviour and Lord, He exchanges your sins for His righteousness, and provides complete cleansing and protection.

(c) New dots are drawn on the laminated paper but are easy to erase.

You sin but, as you repent, your sin is removed immediately .

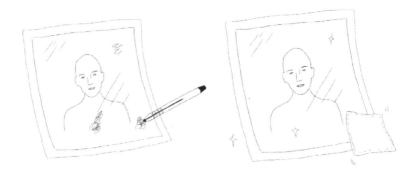

(d) Sticky notes stick to the paper.

Through events in your life and the culture around you, people and society label you, and you label yourself. When you believe these labels, they stick to you.

(e) Cloths replace the sticky notes.

God exchanges these lies for His truth. As you enjoy a daily relationship with God, with the Holy Spirit's help, you become Christlike.

(f) The sticky notes try to stick to the cloths but they can't stick properly.

When you know the truth, the enemy's attempts to reattach his lies to you will end in failure. You will continue to walk in victory. The truth God has spoken to you, which you now believe by faith, will be your shield and protect you from all Satan's attacks (see Ephesians 6.16).

Keep it simple and remember to come to Him

To become a Christian is like becoming a prince or a princess after being a slave. We change from being sinners to saints because Jesus becomes our righteousness, and we become members of God's royal family. However, we often still behave as if we were slaves.

Do we become slaves again because we still behave as slaves? No! We're still members of God's royal family; we're just not fully trained yet. Our starting point is the holiness and righteousness given to us by Jesus. Let's focus on learning more about the role of 'being' who we are, rather than trying to achieve, by our own efforts, what we already are. As the Holy Spirit walks with us step by step, we start to learn how to behave like royal sons and daughters of God, to become more and more like Christ.

So please remember always that you are a saint, because of Jesus Christ, even though you might still be struggling with your problems. Just come to Him and learn from Him. I believe that heaven is a place in which people fully recognize that they can't live without God: while they were on earth, they learned how to rely on God.

We are created to be dependent on God. He satisfies our needs completely but we have declared independence from Him and gone our own way. God is saying to us now:

Everyone who thirsts,
Come to the waters;
And you who have no money,
Come, buy and eat.
Yes, come, buy wine and milk
Without money and without price.
Why do you spend money for what is not bread,
And your wages for what does not satisfy?

Listen carefully to Me, and eat what is good,
And let your soul delight itself in abundance.
Incline your ear, and come to Me.
Hear, and your soul shall live;
And I will make an everlasting covenant with you.
(Isaiah 55:1–3 NKJV)

God's way is very simple but we keep trying to search in other places or for other – more difficult – solutions. God is asking you simply to come to Him. He is offering Himself to you.

May our desire and destiny be to walk with God always and forever. Enjoy this journey with God on earth, and continue it in heaven.

Lightning Source UK Ltd.
Milton Keynes UK
UKHW010933250721
387701UK00001B/68